Tom Three Persons was created as a one-person oral performance piece by Yvonne Trainer in the early 1990's. Yvonne's audiences have variously defined it as a Biography in Verse, a work of Prairie Realism, a Postmodern long poem, a Postcolonial text, and a Multimedia piece. In Yvonne's own words: "Tom Three Persons stands as symbol for my childhood on the Canadian prairie and the death of that childhood." Ultimately, on the page, *Tom Three Persons* reveals the striving to go beyond the self, whatever the situation, toward the advancement of human progress.

Also by Yvonne Trainer:

Manyberries
Customers
Everything Happens at Once
Landscape Turned Sideways: New and Selected

FRONTENAC HOUSE
Calgary

Tom Three Persons

A Multimedia Poetry Sequence
by Yvonne Trainer

Cover and Book Design by EPIX Design Inc.
Cover picture: Tom Three Persons, Glenbow Archives.

Frontenac House acknowledges the support of Alberta Foundation for the Arts.

National Library of Canada Cataloguing in Publication Data

Trainer, Yvonne.
Tom Three Persons

(Quartet 2002)
Poems.
ISBN 0-9684903-8-7

1. Three Persons, Tom, 1888-1949–Poetry. I. Title. II. Series.
PS8589.R3374T65 2002 C811'.54 C2002-910153-0
PR9199.3.T63T65 2002

Printed and bound in Canada

Published by Frontenac House Ltd.
1138 Frontenac Avenue S.W.
Calgary, AB T2T 1B6 Canada
Tel: (403) 245-2491 Fax: (403) 245-2380
E-mail: editor@frontenachouse.com
Website: www.frontenachouse.com

1 2 3 4 5 6 7 8 9 06 05 04 03 02

Acknowledgements

Thanks to the Glenbow Archives for the use of photographs. Full documentation of photographers and subjects for these photographs are available from the Glenbow Museum website: http://www.glenbow.org

Title page and P. 69, Tom Three Persons at Calgary Stampede grounds, 1912. NA-335-79; P. 10, Tom Three Persons, Blood Reserve, Alberta. NA 617-1; P. 30, Program cover, 1912 Calgary Exhibition & Stampede. NA-604-1; P. 33 and cover, Tom Three Persons. NA-778-7; P. 41, Tom Three Persons and little boy. NA-584-1; P. 50, Tom and wife, Tom is wearing his championship medal. NA-689-1; P. 55, Tom Three Persons with little girl, Fort Macleod, Alberta. NA 1137-1.

Thanks also to the Glenbow for the use of the archive materials for letters and newspaper articles which have been edited and sometimes fictionalized to be turned into found poems.

Contents

Tom Three Persons

This long poem sequence deals with the life of Tom Three Persons, a Blood from the Standoff Reserve in Alberta and champion bronco rider of the first Calgary Stampede in 1912. He won the championship on a horse named Cyclone that 126 other cowboys had not been able to ride. He also rode at the Winnipeg Stampede, yearly, and won regularly.

These "feats of Horsemanship" were not his only successes. In the early 20th century, the Standoff Reserve was one of the poorest in Canada; remarkably, though, Tom worked his way through grade 12 at the Dunbar Indian School near Calgary. By the time he died he also owned 200 head of cattle and approximately 50 race horses.

In this sequence of poems, which may be read as individual pieces or as a whole, Tom appears as an Ariel-like figure with a need to tell his story in verse, or at least what he remembers of it. Throughout, he recalls his two sons, Jessie and Jimmy (also known as Wilton). He also remembers his three wives, Ambush Woman, Eliza, and Lily, whom he married within a short time of each other. The last poem recalls his wives in the images of nuns who keep vigil by his deathbed. Failing memory makes these three nuns his wives again who finally fade to three shadows. These wives define the early, middle and last years of Tom's life.

Although my own grandfather was not a Blood but a Blackfoot from the Blackfeet Reservation near Browning, Montana, he shared the Blackfoot language with Tom. Moreover, they died in the same hospital – the Holy Cross Hospital in Calgary – in the same year. My grandfather could not speak except when he put his fingers to the hole in his throat. He was dying from throat cancer. So, perhaps, here Tom speaks for both of them.

Ultimately, this sequence serves as a multi-media piece. The poems and photographs merge, fading in and out, and the poems were originally delivered as a 30-minute recitation.

Yvonne Trainer
Edmonton, 2001

This book is dedicated to the memory
of Tom Three Persons 1886-1949

The poems are dedicated to Ambush Woman, Eliza,
and Lily, and also to Jessie and Jimmy (Wilton)

Where are you going in your feathers and your leathers, Tom?
Where are you going in your feathers and your leathers?
And why so sad, Tom? Why so sad?

Where are you going in your hat and boots, Tom?
Where are you going in your hat and boots?
And why so sad, Tom? Why so sad?

Where are you going in your suit and shoes, Tom?
Where are you going in your suit and shoes?
And why so sad, Tom? Why so sad?

Tom Three Persons

My name is Tom Three Persons
I'm no relation to the American
Tom Three Persons
named because he killed three men
I never killed anyone
nor robbed a bank
nor anything like that
I was named because of three women
mother saw walking past the door
the moment of my birth
Father claimed there were no women
The door was closed
I am not even sure there was a door
I may have been born in a teepee

I was named because we're all named
Because Bloods believe
names float in air

I the receiver
of a name given
I who knew none of this
who crowed myself to sleep
strapped in my cradle board
under the watchful look of crows
I who called their name
before I knew my own.

Mission School/Day One

(Brother)
in the wooden tub
you scrubbed me raw
as a sweet potato

Your shears
like a hawk's beak
snipped my black braids

Breechcloth
and moccasins
torn away

you handed me starched pants
and shirt
and polished shoes

Those pants
scraped like buck brush
against my legs

That collar
strangled my neck
like a snake

I learned to run with shoes of stone

though my feet blistered
read as palms of uncles
peeling bark from cedar posts

you
like the oblate priest and gray nuns
no longer believed

in that room
fully dressed
I stood more exposed.

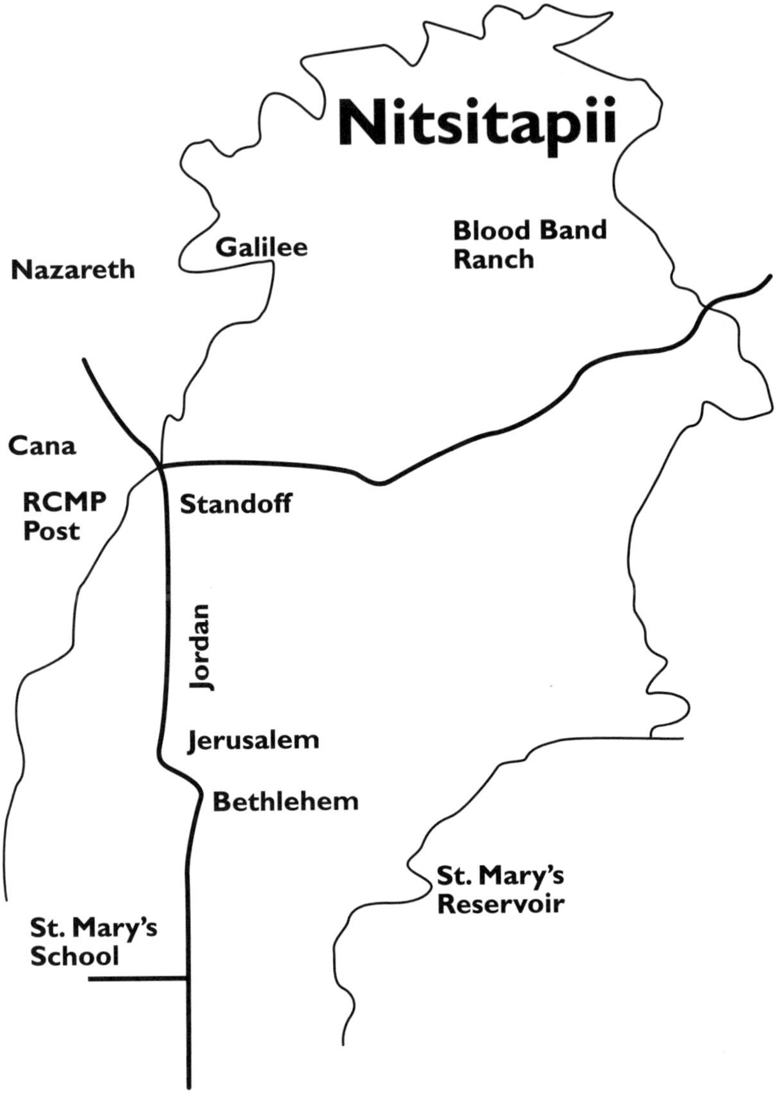
Nitsitapii
Blood Band
Ranch
Galilee
Nazareth
Cana
RCMP
Post
Standoff
Jordan
Jerusalem
Bethlehem
St. Mary's
Reservoir
St. Mary's
School

Nitsitapii

Nazareth Galilee Blood Band Ranch

Cana

RCMP Post   Standoff

J
o
r
d
a
n

Jerusalem
Bethlehem

St. Mary's School   St. Mary's
Reservoir

On the Reserve

On the Reserve
the ponies were so skinny
we could've sharpened our hunting knives
on their ribs

When we walked across prairie
brown grass broke like glass

I sat with cousins
in the shade of my parents' shack
drew picture with a stick
in the dirt

Evenings we built tall fires
to keep away mosquitoes
I watched flames buck
Dreamt of a shiny black horse
and of owning a ranch
The elders told stories
of buffalo hunts
I see my Grandfather ride
to the head of the herd

Arrows
cut across my vision.

The Beginning

Born at the beginning of the beginning
Louis Riel hanged
Poundmaker and Big Bear jailed
Born at the beginning
          of railroads   and fences
          and irrigation ditches
          built like birth canals

Released
          from walls
                    and flesh

No not released
but kicked a way through
wearing rattlesnake boots
and red angora chaps
Slit the umbilical cord
between sharp guns
faster than a rustler cutting fence

No better yet
          rode out of a chute
                    on a shiny black
                              bucking horse

a winner.

Kainai Horse Races

To those who spoke no English
nor followed the white man's calendar
it was moon of the ripe berries

Women and children
went in wagons
to pick branches bare
I went to the Kainai horse races
picked a cayuse
that had never been ridden
Even where there was nothing
to hold on to
and I was somewhere
between
sky and horse
I held on
Reined 'im to the finish

Sun climbed
hawks scattered

Then Jack Low Horn came up
said "Tom
I got bad news
Can't go to Macleod
They won't let Indians
in at the Fair
They say we're a nuisance
They'll even let dogs
onto the grounds
not us"

I turned then
and walked with my shadow
to a hill
I shook my fist hard
It was night then   All summer
it was moon of the dried berries.

Prohibition

(Original story told by Dr. Hugh Dempsey)

It was so dry
wood in the Cardston temple was splintering
Calling High Jack Low Horn and I
went to a bootlegger
but he wouldn't give us liquor
unless we brought him a woman

In the camps below the High Level Bridge
there were women
but none would come with us
so we borrowed a dress
a red one
and Jack Low Horn put it on
and we pulled a scarf way down
over his face
and took him to the bootlegger
and got our jug

Then we ran
but Jack tripped
and the dress tore at the waist
and he swore
so you could hear him all over Lethbridge
Then he was a man again
The bootlegger was a dog

We ran until our chests ached
and our soles burned
Then we hid
in the shadows of the cliff

under the High Level Bridge
and drank the bitter sweetness
like laughter.

Ambush Woman

you set traps for animals
in rock piles

head of weasel
toe of mink
coat of muskrat
legs of fox
shadow of lynx
prowess of bobcat

I am unmarked
when you
set me
free

Fort Macleod RCMP

They came with fists at the door
I lit the coal oil lamp before answering
They said "You're coming with us"

In those days
they'd come and get you
even if it was just a rumour
that you'd been drinking

They let me put on my clothes
Ambush Woman's eyes were shining in the dark
I whispered "Don't forget to feed the yearlings"

What they really wanted
was for me to break the police horses
they'd brought across the border

They took me to the corral by the jail
It was five in the morning
They said "Good Blood"
and I didn't know if they were referring
to the horses or me
but those horses were good all right
big strong ones worth it for a ride

Each day I gave a one-man performance

Nights I slept hard in my cell
        dreamt of larger rodeos
Every prisoner a participant
        crime an event.

Rodeo Talk

Sure it hurts
Torn arm muscles and crack'd ribs
don't heal easy
Darn near can't get my breath
climbin' back on

But I'll stick to 'im this time
It's bin a long summer
thinkin' of how Volcano explodes
thinkin' 'bout the times he's thrown me

But I've got a feelin'
this time'll be different
like when I rode Earthquake
and I was shiver'n all over
shiver'n 'till I got a hot spur in his belly
Then he couldn't shake me

Sure Volcano's a mountain
of movin' flesh
but give me eight seconds
and I'll feel good inside these ribs
and I won't need to move my arm
'cause the wind'll lift my hat
to the crowd.

1912

There is power
in Calgary
Lights in windows
that have nothing to do
with reflections
from moon or stars or sun

Power
in Calgary
and none of it
carried in the bag
of the Medicine Man
or in the wisdom
of the chief

Hydro-electricity
I am told
is as easy to understand
as a current of flowing water
There is power here
In this city it will
never be night again.

Department of Indian Affairs,
June 17th, 1912.

W.J. Hyde, Esq.,
Indian Agent,
Macleod, Alta.

Dear Sir,-

In view of the fact that the Liquor traffic is getting worse year by year among the Indians more or less throughout all the country, the Department has come to the conclusion that the most stringent measures for its suppression must be taken.

I beg to instruct you that in the future you will impose the maximum fine AND imprisonment with hard labour to anyone infringing the Act, of course always using discretion; at the same time always bearing in mind the policy is to frighten the Criminal element from breaking the law in this particular way.

Be good enough to govern yourself according to the instructions in this letter and report to me how it works out.

Yours truly

Glen Campbell
Chief Inspector I.D.
Per. LL

Calgary Stampede, 1912

Indian Affairs and the Stampede Board
gave us transportation
and rationing
gave us a place
by the river
gave us a schedule
of when and where
they wanted us

Painted faces   war-whoops
and feathers
we rode like burning hell
through the streets of Calgary
We were stared at with wonder

and with more than a little fear
We were policed and patrolled
After each show we were sent back
to our place by the river
We were given a curfew

Nights after the fire had been dampened
and the last human shadows
had disappeared into teepees
the river carried the echo of our voices
away from the city.

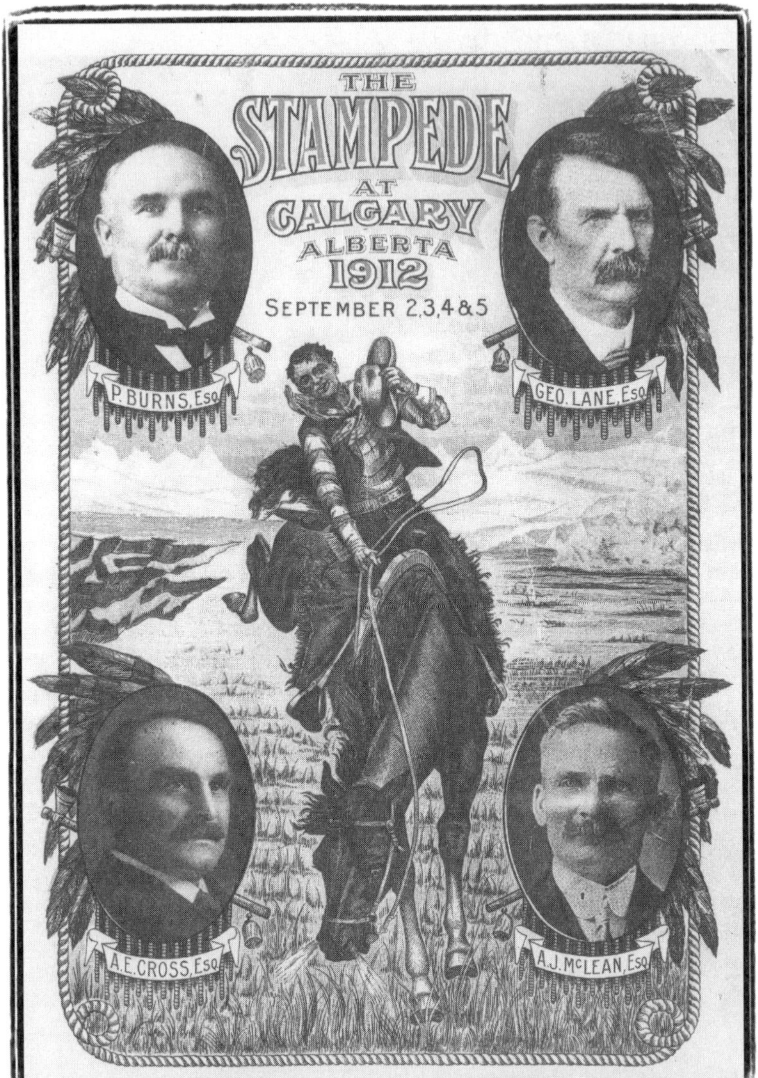
THE
STAMPEDE
AT
CALGARY
ALBERTA
1912
SEPTEMBER 2,3,4 & 5
P. BURNS, Esq.
GEO. LANE, Esq.
A.E. CROSS, Esq.
A.J. McLEAN, Esq.

Bull Rider

Riding the black bull
out of the steel chute
through the iron gate
into the arena
into the eyes
of a thousand people

the pick-up men waiting
stiff as pall-bearers
The judge
bringing the red flag down
while the clown running in
thrusts a bucket under
the bull's nose

Grinning
Miss Lucile Mulhall
closes her eyes and slides off
real slow.

Snapsot

Someone said "like Hollywood"
Someone said "Ya won
Tom ya won" Still I couldn't believe
thought God   it's the fever
sweating like I was
feet on the ground   still
balanced pole on a barrel
knees cloud high   spurs ground in
waiting the next twist of motion

Someone said "Cyclone"
and there was applause
but I thought thunder
the sky being funny
the way it was
Someone said "The Duchess
she's in the grandstand"
and when I looked up

everyone was standing hands clapping
stone to stone
Then I knew
and walked out lake-quiet
into the shadows
of the motor-cars

but someone with a box camera
came and drew me into the sun
and I couldn't help
smiling a little
when he snapped this picture.

Calgary Daily Herald

Calgary, Alberta. Wednesday, September 11, 1912

DUKE OF CONNAUGHT
CONGRATULATES INDIAN

Glen Campbell, chief inspector of Indian Agencies, has received a telegram from the equerry of His Royal Highness the Duke of Connaught dated at Banff to the following effect:

"Please convey his Royal Highness's congratulations to Tom Three Persons on his feat of horsemanship."

Praise

Do those who praise me
believe
praise means anything?

I know the horses I've ridden
I know the ones I haven't.

Blood Agency,
Macleod Alta.
September 17, 1912.

Glen Campbell, Esq.
Indian Department,
Winnipeg, Man.

Dear Mr. Campbell,

* * *

I presume you have seen the reports in the paper regarding Tom Three Persons to the effect that you bailed him out of gaol to give him the opportunity to ride, after riding he went back to gaol and you handed the Royal Hig[h]ness' congratulations through the bars of his cell. Immediately on seeing it I wrote to Mr Collin McLeod to make the newspapers publishing the report apologise, but as yet I have not heard the result.

* * *

I remain,
Yours very sincerely,

W.J. Hyde,
Indian Agent.
WJH/OKU.

Instructions for Living in Jail

Caged up like a dog
gnaw at the bars
bark at the kid
in the next cage

who speaks neither blackfoot
nor english
norwegian maybe
growl at the guard
In your ears
          a river
List'n
like a dog
head cocked
eyes wide

scratch a little
behind one ear or the other
like coyote in the spring

piss in a hole
curl up on cold dirt floor
night frozen your hair.

Chant for Three Voices

Hi Ya!
Crop Ear Wolf
Wolf Bull
Running Crane
Many Dust
One Spot
Old Moon
Running Wolf
Hi Yah!
Eagle Rib
Heavy Shield
Bull Horn
Many Horses
Running Deer
Bull Shield
Hi Ya!
Hi Yah!
Hiiiiiiiiiiii yah!

Hi Ya!
Wolf Bull
Running Crane
Many Dust
One Spot
Old Moon
Running Wolf
Eagle Rib
Hi Yah!
Heavy Shield
Bull Horn
Many Horses
Running Deer
Bull Shield
Crop Ear Wolf
Hi Ya!

Hi Ya!
Running Crane
Many Dust
One Spot
Old Moon
Running Wolf
Eagle Rib
Heavy Shield
Hi Yah!
Bull Horn
Many Horses
Running Deer
Bull Shield
Crop Ear Wolf
Wolf Bull
Hi Yah!

Learning the Language

What kind of life
was that? Jimmy
at St. Paul's Mission School
bent like a question mark
in a desk
writing
"I must not speak Blackfoot"
one hundred times
every time his tongue slipped

At that school he learned
a powerful new language

silence.

Where Ever I Went

Where ever I went
children followed

They shook my hand
They stood beside me
to measure themselves
They held my medals
rubbed smooth as stones
in the Belly River

I was not yet old
I did not talk
of Winter's blizzard
lack of medicine
hunger   Most of them
knew this anyway

I did not tell them
joy of bad liquor
in the gut
and once my own son led me
strong-willed through bunch grass
to this secret place
by the river
Our shadows fell
we stood still
Ripples wrinkled our faces
The distance could not hold us

We threw our bodies
like stones to the water
We fought our way up
Shirts stuck to shoulder blades
hair matted against foreheads
we sought each other.

A Shadow on This Hour

Can it be memory
that throws a shadow
on this hour?

Just past Carnellie's
Sporting Goods
I think
        of all those guns

pointed in the direction
of the mounted heads
Of hooks

ready to be baited
and cast out
into Summer waters

I turn to the hills
where deer graze
A bird whistles

Among trees
          Billy Manyfingers –
                    ten years old

carves inches deep
into wood
that will not heal

Better not to think
when walking
Better just to walk

with the birdwatchers
looking for bright flickers
in high branches

or to stroll along the river
with the children
Always in the shadows

speaking to a shadow.

Blood Agency,
Macleod. Alta.
August 4. 1913.

Glen Campbell, Esq.
Chief Inspector, Indian Agencies.
winnipeg [sic]. Man.

Dear Mr Campbell,

Tom Three Persons was here today, and wished me to write and explain to you, why it is that he is not now going to Winnipeg to again win the Championship. He was over at Harlen on the other side of the line, the beginning of last month, when they got him to give an exhibition ride, the mare after doing her prettiest Stampeded and ran into a wash-out, coming a cropper and falling on Tom, hurting his back rather badly, so not feeling fit, he decided not to go to winnipeg [sic]. He was also afraid that you might have heard that he had been thrown off while over there, but he desires me to explain that he was giving an exhibition ride and the Managers over there offered him $25.00 to ride and Fifty if he get [sic] thrown off, so the fifty looked good to him after riding the horse almost to a quit he fell off, but he says the amount of jeering he had to undergo there is no horse will ever repeat the trick. He regrets very much not being able to go but desires his kind remembrances to Guy Weadick and yourself. Hope our Indians will behave themselves and make a gay appearance. It was rather an inconvenient time to send them not only are we in the middle of haying but the Macleod fair is on, and as are [sic] Indians had already made a number of entries, one or two of our best outfits had made entries at the fair here and consequently could not go to winnipeg [sic]. With best wishes, for a successful Stampede.

Yours very sincerely,

W.J. Hyde,
Indian Agent

Came to Me

Came to me in the middle of the night
didn't want to be a cowboy anymore
wanted to be Doc Edwards
wanted to wear little round lenses
in gold frames
a white coat
soft soles

Came to me I knew what it was like
14 hours a day   pain   every muscle aching
shoulders half-pulled from sockets
The horse jerking its head
So many bloody mosquitoes

Rodeoing every summer
paying more for the entry fee
than I won

Came to me   sprained knee
broken ribs   cracked collarbone

Came to me then
the tiredness in Doc's eyes
his searching probing
The patients he saw every day
The times he fixed them up
though they had nothing to give
The ones he couldn't save from pain

In This Instant

In this instant
I see what brought me
to this piece of land
I talk to the Indian Agent
I purchase it

I have always said
"If I could find it"

Now that I have
I dig a well
for stars to fall into

for the St. Mary's
to flow through
for the hand to cup

for the bucket to rust in
for winter to freeze
for spring to break through

Winter Skies

Winter skies are moonfull
Roads go nowhere
Rocks sleep

Beneath a wooden marker
bones of Ambush Woman
wait

Years now

Hills keep the silence
Sometimes wind speaks.

Summer Long

All summer long
I sleep under stars

coyote's eyes watch

light clouds
dreams scrape silence

dense scrub-brush
fans the creek
and a skinny stallion
stands up
to sleep.

The New Coupe

The new coupe set in the shed
like a shiny coin
Jimmy couldn't keep his hands off
Nights when Jessie and I
drank ourselves to our knees
he'd put a comb in the ignition
start it
Go for a joy ride

Each night he'd drive back late
push the coupe inside

One night he pushed too hard

next morning I looked out the window
said "What's happened to the shed?"
There was a hole bigger than a man
right through the other side

Jimmy just paced
round the kitchen
his hair messed up
hands in pockets
comb digging
into his fingers

Jessie and I used to fight
with fists like iron
but I never hit Jimmy
Didn't have to
My voice was enough.

For Eliza

Sweet petals
or shadowy music
Tired skies
Mosses creep
Flowers sleep

We who moan sorrow
fold from slumber's spirit
enjoy toil

In the wind's green noon
dew falls sweetened
the autumn days flower
and in the dark why
                        life alone

Climbing
  toward
    silence
      and
wedded embraces
warm our strange ghosts.

At the Hot Springs

There were wooden legs
and hooks that worked
like arms
left unguarded
while bodies swam
to heal themselves

I came to relax
Still my bones ached
in the heaviness of water
I had arms   legs   a complete body
though my joints moved slowly
like blades of a rusted Model T fan

Jimmy and Jessie
wouldn't come in
Stood poised like birds on shore
laughed at their old man

The water was too hot
I got out fast

Then it was autumn
and beginning to snow
We headed for Vancouver
I was still looking for summer.

Vancouver

I'd never seen that much water before
Not even in Spring
when the St. Mary's Dam flooded
The ocean made me think of prairie grass in the wind
We took off our boots and waded in
I remember the story of coyote
with a seashell around its neck
I was that coyote limping along

Coyote pretending to limp raced the man
Half-way round coyote lost his limp and won

My limp is real
There was nothing at the end of the trail
The seagulls kept shitting on everything
I thought of the beauty of magpies
Every day we went down to the ocean
Every day we got lost reading signs in Vancouver
looking for a café and a liquor store.

Flying Devil

(For Jimmy)

Remember
that little pony
we called Flyin' Devil?

You'd ride 'im
round the yard
like a sheep
but put a flank strap on 'im
he'd buck through the sky

He threw the dude cowboy on the fence
broke his back
spectators screamed

and after I rode up
took the flank strap off
said "You ride 'im out of the corral"

You were just a little fella then
but you jumped on
rode 'im
gentle as summer
through the gate
got off   crawled under his belly
half-dozen times
lifted a hoof

That fella
with the broken back screaming

you standing there
grinnin'
gettin' all the attention.

Oil Boom

Whitewashed house
Chicken pecking garbage
Lazy Saint Mary's river

beyond the dam
oil wells sprouting
like big steel cacti
out of land
            forms
            silence

dark sky
and black roads
where trucks go
            sometimes

Steel blades
grinding through earth-
bone

another
giant badger
hole

and
no
oil.

Cards

I have two aces and a six
in my hand
I don't even remember
the rules of the game

All I remember is
Jack Low Horn and Calling High
stayed half the winter
We lived inside
dreading early morning cold
and evening
and chores   And in between
we played poker

All I know is
supplies were getting low
All I know is
I had to win
because the one who lost
did the chores.

Horses at Night

When I hear horses whinnying in the night
and chomping grass outside my window
I feel as though I'm in a tent
horses staked out behind still sweaty
the stains on their backs and underbellies
the shape of a saddle and cinch

They shy when sudden wind shakes the clothes
strung on a line between trees   A tent
keeps nothing out except mosquitoes
                                        sometimes.

The Mind is the Place

The mind is the place the heart turns to
when it has fallen out of its nest

The heart is the one who walks heartless
along the Belly River or through prairie grass
or in another country or perhaps in its own country

The heart is the one who is

among the senses: clover
and mint and sweet grass
or in this province sagebrush perhaps

The eye is the place of the mind
the retina stretched to its limit –
a hole in the old dark blanket

The mind is the heart is the eye is
the nest is broken: twigs mud   grass.

Ask

Ask
why I live
on the prairie

I laugh
and walk
into silence

Yellow leaves
in a dry creek bed
lie undisturbed.

Sonnet

(for Lily)

man
woman
potato patch
mosquitoes
stars
but cold could
end
all

Touch me
I live
now
to love then
this one
felt splendor.

It's the Hour

It's the hour
when Orange Cat
comes out of the shadows and rolls like a moon
in the dark grass

the hour when a door bangs
when the twitter of birds falls from roofs into hedges
when the hospital fills with the oh oh oh of pain
and the nurse delivers pills in white thimbles
and there's that waiting for something
                                                            or someone
perhaps

the hour when the paw of a white lion
stretches like a nurse's sleeve into shadows
of a room where there are no lions
and for a second there is something –
a pain like a claw hammer
in the chest

and in these iron beds
the sick ones sink back   exhausted but alert
into the grey   into themselves

while Orange Cat keeps rolling and rolling
almost as far as Fort Macleod   as if
that's what cats are supposed to do

and the sick ones sink deeper
into the purr of prairie grass
quietly and barely breathing   listening.

And the nurse leaning forward asks:
"Tom, where is home?"

It's a whitewashed ranch house
Half an hour ride
west of Spring Coulee
Inside there are hides
on the walls
antelope and cow
a skin of a bobcat I shot
because its one leg had been torn off
There's a stuffed dog named Shep
that belonged to Jimmy
Lily threatens to throw it out
because it loses hair
There is a pot-belly stove
and a woodstove
that crackles
like crunch of boots
on snow

There is a window to the east
Out of it
I can see the racetrack
where horses run in the summer
I hear them thundering

now.

August 1949

Three nuns keep vigil by the bed
Burn candles
into the night
carry rosary beads
that look like seeds
of gardens in spring
though by now it must be autumn

Ambush Woman leaning over
to weed carrots
How many years' moons
did I plough stalks under?

This land is damn hard

Eliza picking bugs
from potato plants
the crows gather and bunch up
So many years' moons
I ploughed stalks under
Lily hoeing potatoes
into the night
Candles burn like fireflies
Become hard stars

The Doctor will not come
'til morning.

Now
I'm riding away from the ranch
I look back
Ambush Woman!
I look again
Eliza!
I look again
Lily!

The horse is running faster faster
its ears plastered to its head
like a donkey
my stubborn refusal to let go

The distance cannot hold me
I look back

On the whitewashed wall
three shadows
passing.

Classic Stampede Ride Of Tom Three Persons On "Cyclone" Recalled
-Funeral At Cardston

August 1949:

Though the earth will close over the remains of Tom Three Persons today at Cardston, the legend of his fabulous feats as a bronc buster will live on.

Tom Three Persons was one of the original Calgary Stampeders back in 1912. When the great Alberta cattlemen got together and offered a $100,000 jackpot for the first stampede cowboys, who came from as far away as Mexico to try for the gold.

Then as now the bronc riding competition was the number one event, most thrilling breath-taking show of all. And despite the terrific competition all the glory went to Tom Three Persons. Big Tom drew the toughest bucking horse of all time - Cyclone - when the last day rolled around.

Gets Ovation

Thousands stood on their feet to give a tremendous ovation - not to the highly reputed visitors from across the border, but to a hard-riding, devil-may-care Alberta Indian, Tom Three Persons of the Bloods, who rode to a finish on Cyclone, still rated the greatest outlaw bronco of them all.

The Cardston Cowboy came back often to succeeding Calgary Stampedes after the event was revived in 1919. But he never again reached the pinnacle he achieved the day he rode Cyclone into the ground.

Along with other veteran riders Tom Three Persons was a visitor at times at the Lethbridge rodeo when his days as an active rider had passed. Today there are only two cowboys left of the number who competed in Calgary in 1912: Clem Gardner, of Pincher Creek, and Irby Mundy, out of Shamrock, Texas.

Tom Three Persons' ride was one of the greatest of all time. He'll always be remembered as the man who tamed Cyclone.

Throngs at Funeral

CARDSTON-(HNS)- St. Mary's R.C. church on the Blood Reserve was thronged Wednesday morning for the funeral of the late Tom Three Persons, famous Indian Rodeo star and stockman. Indians and white friends attended the service, part of which was in Blackfoot tongue.

Rev. Fr. Frapprere and Rev. Fr. LaVern officiated, the latter giving the funeral sermon. He has been a missionary among the Bloods for over 50 years.

The noted stampede rider was buried with the medal and belt he received at the Calgary Stampede in 1912. Pallbearers were S. O. And J. S. Low, Hebert Matkin, Frank Card, V. Hillmer, Joe Crowfoot, Charlie Royal and Steve Fox Jr. Joe Crowfoot and Charlie Royal are from the Blackfoot Reserve, Gleichen. Burial was in the Indian Cemetery on the Reserve.

LET 'ER BUCK
"THE STAMPEDE" CALGARY. ALTA 1912
OFFICIAL PHOTO No 46.
MARCELL

The Listening Fire

By the listening fire
a drummer
puts sticks to stretched canvas
paints music
Yellow moccasins
pad the earth
Young Bloods dance
the dance of the blood

Dogs sniff the night

A deaf-dumb moon
lip-reads mouths
of shadows.

Where are you going in your feathers and your leathers, Tom?
Where are you going in your feathers and your leathers?
And why so sad, Tom? Why so sad?

Going to buy a hat. Going to buy boots.
Going to the rodeo to ride a horse you know

You walked in your feathers and your leathers before, Tom
You walked in your feathers and your leathers before
Why not now, Tom? Why not now?

Where are you going in your hat and boots, Tom?
Where are you going in your hat and boots?
And why so sad, Tom? Why so sad?

Going to buy a suit. Going to buy shoes.
Going to give a speech because I won the rodeo

You spoke in your hat and your boots before, Tom
You spoke in your hat and your boots before
Why not now, Tom? Why not now?

Where are you going in your suit and shoes, Tom?
Where are you going in your suit and shoes?
And why so sad, Tom? Why so sad?

Yvonne Trainer was born in 1959 and raised south of Manyberries, Alberta as an only child, 32 miles from the nearest neighbour. She holds a BASc (English) from the University of Lethbridge, an MA in (English /Creative Writing) from the University of New Brunswick, and is completing the final year of a PhD program from the University of Manitoba. Her PhD studies are primarily focused on Contemporary Canadian and American poetry with a special area of interest in Canadian Literature and Medicine. Yvonne has published one chapbook and three books of poetry: *Manyberries, Customers* (Fiddlehead Books), *Everything Happens at Once* (Fiddlehead Books), and *Landscape Turned Sideways: New and Selected* (Goose Lane).